BOOK ANALYSIS

By Hudson Cleveland

The Man in the High Castle

BY PHILIP K. DICK

Bright
≡Summaries.com

ANALYSIS   48&

FURTHER REFLECTION   49

FURTHER READING   53

PHILIP K. DICK

AMERICAN NOVELIST

- **Born in Chicago, Illinois, in 1928.**
- **Died in Santa Ana, California, in 1982.**
- **Notable works:**
  - *Do Androids Dream of Electric Sheep?* (1968), novel
  - *Ubik* (1969), novel
  - *A Scanner Darkly* (1977), novel

Philip K. Dick is one of the most influential sci-fi writers of all time, as well as one of the most prolific. With over two dozen novels and over 100 short stories published in his lifetime, Dick's fiction explores dense philosophical subjects. Perhaps most notable and most frequent among them were metaphysics and the nature of reality, as well as what constitutes a real human being in worlds increasingly dominated by virtual reality, androids, and commercialisation.

While not enormously successful while he was alive, Dick's novels have been adapted into numerous critically acclaimed films (such as *Blade Runner* [1982] and *Total Recall* [1990, 2012]), and his works are typically regarded as foundational to the sci-fi genre.

THE MAN IN THE HIGH CASTLE

IN AN ALTERNATE FUTURE WHERE THE AXIS POWERS WON WWII, THE DISTINCTION BETWEEN REAL AND COPY IS BLURRING

- **Genre:** science fiction novel
- **Reference edition:** Dick, P. K. (2015) *The Man in the High Castle*. London: Penguin Classics.
- **1st edition:** 1962
- **Themes:** international conflict, science fiction, reality, simulacra, postwar fiction, WWII, paranoia, nationalism, national consciousness

In the 1960s in what used to be the United States, Japan and Germany have divided the continent into territories. The mysterious Mr Baynes arrives in San Francisco, California, Japanese territory, under the pretence of being a salesman. His presence, however, signals and catalyses a conflict between Germany and Japan. Caught in the wake of this international conflict are Frank

Frink, his ex-wife Juliana, and Robert Childan, and the events engender two questions: what is real, and who is the man in the High Castle?

SUMMARY

POSTWAR AMERICA AND VINTAGE AMERICANA

Robert Childan, owner of an antiques store, gets a call from one Mr Tagomi, who is frustrated that a poster he had ordered has yet to arrive. After Childan suggests some replacement pieces, a young Japanese couple comes in and he manages to make himself feel better by easily making a sale.

Frank 'Goldfish' Frink lays in bed late into the morning. He lives on the West Coast of what used to be the United States – after Capitulation Day in 1947, some parts of the continent came under the control of Japan, and others of the German Third Reich. As a Jewish man in hiding, Frink thinks he must either "come to terms" (p. 18) with his employer Wyndam-Matson or the Japanese authorities – any other options would push him into German territory, where he would be at risk of death if his identity were discovered. Along with the victory of the Axis powers in WWII, we learn that Germany "wiped out" (p. 17) Africa and made it into a slave colony.

Frink consults his copy of the *I Ching – The Book of Changes*, a Taoist oracle-text – to find out how best to talk to Wyndam-Matson, as well as whether he will ever see his ex-wife Juliana again. The oracle suggests modesty for the former, and that Juliana was not meant for him, even though he still loves her.

Nobusuke Tagomi consults his own *I Ching* to discern how his meeting will go with his client, Mr Baynes, to whom he was meant to give Childan's late antique. Tagomi calls in Mr Ramsey, a man of Midwest United States descent, to properly judge the authenticity of the replacement artefacts Childan will bring. The oracle predicts that the meeting with Baynes will go well, and Tagomi infers that a working relationship beneficial to his business will be struck up. The oracle also reveals that Baynes is a spy – but for whom, Tagomi cannot discern.

ARRIVAL IN SAN FRANCISCO

Childan arrives at the Nippon Times Building in San Francisco with the new antique, a Volume One, Number One copy of *Tip Top Comics*. While Childan waits to find a black slave-porter to take his luggage, he reflects on his entry into the antiques business. Following a meeting with an ex-Army man, Major Ito Humo, he learns of the Japanese fascination with niche Americana. He "by stages [...] got into the business" as he realised the value of his American, "historically firsthand account" (p. 32) of these pieces of vintage culture.

Juliana Frink, living as a judo instructor in Colorado, gets into a discussion about race relations at a hamburger restaurant with two truck drivers and the fry cook. Things start to get heated between the truckers and the cook, but Juliana smooths things over. She reflects on the Nazis, who are now spreading their empire to the moon and Mars.

Mr Baynes arrives in San Francisco aboard a German rocket ship. He gets into a conversation about art with a young German next to him. Baynes professes a love for abstract art, but the German, named Alex Lotze, himself produces idealistic Nazi realism, which eschews 'decadence'. As the conversation continues with ostensible amiability, Baynes grows increasingly irked at Lotze's racist commentary. He reflects deeply on the psychology of the Nazi warmongering, imperial mind. As the two debark, Baynes confesses to Lotze – who has claimed a racial kinship to him – that he is Jewish, and that he is in fact one of many secret Jews who operate in the upper echelons of Nazi society, thus immunising him from any reporting on Lotze's part. He seems to do this merely to antagonise Lotze.

Baynes meets Tagomi, who gifts him the antique he has just acquired from Childan: a 1938 Mickey Mouse watch.

NEW BUSINESS VENTURES

Frink goes to the W.-M. Corporation — ostensibly a business which creates fixtures for new apartment buildings, but which also churns out ersatz American antiques and artefacts — to ask his employer Wyndam-Matson for his job back. Wyndam-Matson informs him, however, that he has already been replaced. The shop foreman, Ed McCarthy, suggests that Frink should create custom jewellery with his forgery skills. Frink initially rejects the idea, but consults the *I Ching* and, based on its favourable fortune, returns to McCarthy and agrees that the business venture would be a smart move. McCarthy then quits and joins the endeavour.

Childan is visited by a man looking to buy thousands of dollars' worth of Civil War relics for his boss, Admiral Harusha. Childan shows him a rifle, but the man points out that it is a fake, and leaves, disappointed. Childan frenziedly makes some calls: he discovers that the gun was indeed artificially aged, but also that the man was an impostor. He begins tracing where the gun came from, starting with his supplier Ray Calvin, to locate the source of the forgeries, and to find out how extensively they have spread through his store.

While Wyndam-Matson is entertaining a young woman at his apartment, he receives a call from Ray Calvin, who relays Childan's frenzied concern with fakes. Calvin says that the quality of the fakes is an issue. Wyndam-Matson thinks Frink and McCarthy have something to do with the problem, but cannot pinpoint how. After he ends the call with Calvin, Wyndam-Matson has a conversation about authenticity with the woman he is cheating on his wife with.

Baynes and Tagomi talk about a mysterious third party who will be coming to join in their deliberations. Baynes thinks that Tagomi might be aware that he is secretly a Jew, and regrets having antagonised Lotze.

BUREAUCRATIC CHANGES IN GERMANY

Juliana returns home from grocery shopping to find Joe Cinnadella, the Italian trucker, still asleep in her bed. He has been left behind by his partner, evidently a usual pattern between the two — Joe plans to wait for him when he drives the same way on his return.

Juliana learns of Joe's involvement in the German-Italian campaign in Cairo. The two talk about *The Grasshopper Lies Heavy*, a banned fiction novel in Joe's possession detailing an alternate history wherein the Axis powers lose WWII. Juliana has trouble pinpointing Joe's feelings regarding the war, Germans, Jews, and international conflict. The two listen to a radio program, which announces that Chancellor Bormann, Hitler's successor, has died.

Tagomi has learned that Baynes is not actually Swedish. He is rushed to attend a conference regarding who will replace Chancellor Bormann, but grows ill partway through and leaves early. Baynes calls him when he has returned to his office to ask whether the third party, Mr Yatabe, has contacted him yet. Tagomi relays that he has not.

Frink and McCarthy have successfully appealed to Wyndam-Matson for funds for their new business, and begin working on it immediately.

THE MAN IN THE HIGH CASTLE

Childan goes to dinner with the Kasouras, the young Japanese couple who had patronised his store. Though the conversation occasionally grows tense as Childan has difficulty navigating what exactly they approve of in terms of politics, he enjoys the food and strikes up a successful relationship with the couple. They recommend to him the *Grasshopper* novel, which he assumes crafts a dystopia out of a world run by the victorious Allied powers. When he returns home, waiting for him is a '*pinoc*', a police officer installed by the occupying Japanese government. He questions Childan about the man who had called out the faked antiques at his store. The *pinoc* says that the man's name is Frank Frink.

Hugo Reiss, the Reichs Consul in San Francisco, works busily in the consulate as the world continues to buzz with the decision of the new Chancellor's appointment. Reiss, however, just wants to finish his book — a copy of the *Grasshopper* — and reads it at every moment he can steal away. Though a German, he is utterly fascinated by the book's concepts, and it triggers in him a Nazi paranoia: he wonders angrily, then decides that the author must be Jewish. He almost issues a search for him, as he is purportedly hiding in his 'High Castle' in Wyoming, but decides against it, leaving it to a higher-up if they are so inclined.

EDFRANK JEWELLERY

After two weeks of diligent preparation, Frink and McCarthy are set to sell their wares, christening their business 'Edfrank'. Their aim is to undermine the antiquing businesses by pointing out, as Frink did at Childan's, the fake products — and then to supply their new, contemporary, handwrought pieces and create and corner the market on them.

Cinnadella and Juliana make plans to go on a trip together.

McCarthy attempts to sell jewellery to Childan, but Childan convinces him to leave some on consignment instead — a win-win business scenario for Childan.

Baynes frets over Yatabe's absence, and finally Tagomi's impatience at having to wait for the third party drives Baynes to secretly check Yatabe's progress to San Francisco. A contact undercover at the Fuga Department Store tells him to return the following day to be updated.

ON TO CHEYENNE, WYOMING, AND FRINK AND BAYNES ARE DISCOVERED

Juliana reads *The Grasshopper* while Joe drives them to Denver. The two talk about the book, and Joe rambles about the Italian Fascist 'theory of action'. After realising that Abendsen's 'High Castle' is relatively close by, the two decide to see if they can secure an audience with the mysterious author.

Tagomi receives word from Yatabe himself that he has arrived. He informs Baynes, who excitedly decides to skip his meeting with the department store contact.

Reiss is informed of a political dissident and spy, Rudolf Wegener — the true identity of Baynes — by a German police official, Kreuz vom Meere. The department store contact Baynes met was evidently a double agent working for Germany. Reiss is ordered to arrange Baynes' capture, and newly appointed Chancellor Goebbels calls to directly confirm vom Meere's order.

Childan meets Paul Kasoura to discuss the jewellery. Kasoura describes how he at first laughed at the piece, but quickly became mesmerised and impressed by its artistry and authenticity. He suggests that Childan mass market them, but Childan, sensing that the business offer was a subtle way for the Japanese to make American culture worthless through self-commercialisation, finally declines.

Frink, frustrated by the business' apparent failure, quits. On his way out, he is arrested for conning Childan — and for being Jewish.

YATABE'S ARRIVAL AND THE SIEGE OF THE NIPPON TIMES BUILDING

Yatabe finally arrives at Tagomi's office, and Tagomi quickly realises that he is General Tedeki, the former Imperial Chief of Staff of Japan. Baynes arrives, and delineates to Tedeki the German Reich programme Löwenzahn (or, Dandelion), a false flag operation with the actual intent of a nuclear attack on the Japanese Home Islands. Baynes and Tedeki are discussing plans to subvert the operation now that Goebbels has obtained the chancellorship when German blackshirts assault the building to kidnap Baynes. They are successfully repelled, with Tagomi killing two, but leave no connection to the Reich, and thus no outward way for Japan to condemn the Nazis.

NEARING THE HIGH CASTLE

Joe buys Juliana an overabundance of clothes in Denver, and seems aloof. Juliana realises, when they have made it to their hotel room, that he is on a mission to assassinate Abendsen. Joe has brought her along as Abendsen is purportedly attracted to women just like her. Juliana has an anxiety attack, and manages to cut Joe's carotid artery with a razor blade. She leaves the hotel promising to get help, but flees, and calls the Abendsen residence to ask if she may visit them. She plans to warn the author of the danger.

TAGOMI'S REFLECTIONS ON DEATH

Tagomi wanders the city and reflects on the men he killed in self-defence. He attempts to sell his gun back to Childan, who refuses and instead offers him one of the Edfrank jewellery pieces. Tagomi almost sees what Childan and Kasoumi saw in them, but seems to fall short. He returns to the Nippon Times Building and reprimands the German Consul, Reiss, before having a heart attack. Frink is released from custody without any reason, and returns to work with McCarthy.

BAYNES CAPTURED

Baynes, under the new alias Conrad Goltz, flies back to Germany, where he is arrested. He hopes that Tedeki will manage to disrupt Operation

Dandelion, or that the Nazi war machine will destroy itself by internecine conflict at some indistinct future point.

Juliana learns by newspaper that Joe has been found dead. She finishes *The Grasshopper* when she arrives in Cheyenne, Wyoming, where Abendsen lives.

THE MAN IN THE HIGH CASTLE AND THE REAL WORLD

She arrives at the Abendsen household, and is surprised to find that it is not a 'High Castle' or fortress, as is popularly believed — it is but a normal suburban building, unguarded. She meets Hawthorne Abendsen, the author of *The Grasshopper*, and tells him that she has puzzled out the novel: it was written using the *I Ching*. Using the *I Ching* with Abendsen and his household guests as witnesses, Juliana asks what they are meant to learn from the novel; they discover in asking this question that the novel is true, and that in reality, Germany and Japan lost the war. Juliana leaves, thinking that perhaps she might go back to Frink.

CHARACTER STUDY

FRANK FRINK

After changing his name from Frank Fink to avoid persecution for his Judaism, Frink works for years making forgeries of antique American artefacts. He quits to go into business creating custom, original jewellery with the foreman of his employer, Ed McCarthy, undermining the antique Americana market in the process. He often consults the *I Ching* for guidance, and is ex-husband to Juliana, whom he still yearns for.

Frink has no overt bearing on the narrative, which itself focuses on a mounting international crisis. However, his hand in the creation of forgeries allows for one of the most direct commentaries on 'authentic' versus 'forged'. His connections to Childan and Juliana, and by extension to Tagomi, Baynes, Abendsen, and many others, tie his rather straightforward story of individualism and freedom from commercialisation to the larger story involving international actors.

Frink's business venture with McCarthy represents a revitalisation of authentic artistic works free from commercial interest and mass production.

ROBERT CHILDAN

Childan owns a store renowned for its antique Americana, popular amongst the Japanese population of the occupied American territories. A frantic man interested in big sales, he grows increasingly worried when the authenticity of his works is called into question. He has a major point of contact with the Kasoura couple, who inadvertently help him realise that he was complicit in the trivialisation of American culture.

RUDOLF WEGENER (MR BAYNES)

A spy operating within the German Reich, Wegener disguises himself as a Swiss businessman under the pretence of selling 'injector moulds' to Tagomi in order to warn the Japanese authorities of Operation Dandelion, a German plot to unleash a nuclear assault on the Japanese Home Islands. Wegener grows increasingly worried at the tardiness of the Japanese medium, General Tedeki, but otherwise appears capable under duress. He confesses that he operates as an individual, not working for any agency but guided only by his own moral judgment.

NOBUSUKE TAGOMI

A Japanese businessman working in the Nippon Times Building, Tagomi is the alibi for the meeting between Tedeki and Baynes. Like many of the Japanese characters in the novel, he relies on the *I Ching* for guidance in his life, but when he kills two men to save one — Baynes — his Buddhist-Japanese mindset does not know how to reconcile the imbalance between lives lost and saved. He seems, however, to begin to find solace in the balance in Edfrank artisan works.

JULIANA FRINK

Juliana works as a judo instructor in Colorado, and is described as beautiful and of "Middle-Eastern or Mediterranean" (p. 202) complexion. After meeting Joe Cinnadella, she learns of *The Grasshopper Lies Heavy*, a novel by Hawthorne Abendsen which depicts an alternate history wherein the Axis powers lost the war; she quickly grows fascinated by the book. She has a strong devotion to the *I Ching*, so much so that she is the only one to discover that *The Grasshopper Lies Heavy* was written purely through the fortune-telling text.

Juliana has a desire for relationship that eventually led to her joining with Joe Cinnadella, despite abusive warning signs. Despite Joe's purported history, which is violent and fascistic, she has little trouble condemning Italian and German fascism.

HUGO REISS

Reiss is the Reichs Consul in San Francisco. He is ordered to organise the raid on the Nippon Times Building, and becomes subject to Tagomi's ire for it.

Even though it is an anti-Nazi text, Reiss is one of many who is enthralled by *The Grasshopper Lies Heavy*.

GENERAL TEDEKI (YATABE)

Tedeki is the 'third party' meeting with Tagomi and Baynes. He is the former Imperial Chief of Staff of Japan, acting as ambassador for the Japanese government to collect Baynes' intelligence report on Operation Dandelion.

ED MCCARTHY

McCarthy is the one to suggest that Frink create a new market for original works, and helps him do so with the business venture 'Edfrank'. Although skilled at creating jewellery and a jovial, talkative person, McCarthy is an awkward salesman, and drafts a poor consignment deal with their one successful point of contact, Childan.

PAUL AND BETTY KASOURA

The Kasouras are a young Japanese couple who patronise Childan's store. Childan strikes up a casual relationship with the couple, wherein he attempts to leverage further business. Although they are a seemingly typical Japanese couple, Paul skilfully and subtly manoeuvres Childan into disavowing — and then reaffirming — American artistic ability.

HAWTHORNE ABENDSEN

Abendsen is the author of *The Grasshopper Lies Heavy*, an alternate history wherein the Axis powers lost the war, that might actually constitute reality. He lives with his family in an unassuming house, despite popular rumour that he lives in a fortress-like 'High Castle', and seems unconcerned that one day he might be killed by the Nazis for his writing.

JOE CINNADELLA

Joe Cinnadella is a Swiss man disguised as an Italian trucker, assigned to assassinate Abendsen. He convinces Juliana to accompany him to Denver, Colorado, and then Cheyenne, Wyoming, under the pretence of a vacation — the actual reason being that it is rumoured that Abendsen is attracted to women who look like her, that is, those of a "Middle-Eastern or Mediterranean" (p. 202) complexion. Joe is killed by Juliana after she discovers his true intentions.

ANALYSIS

'AUTHENTIC' AND 'FORGERY'

One of Philip K. Dick's favourite themes, the novel's primary exploration is of the distinction between something which is 'real' and something which is merely a copy of reality — but virtually indistinguishable from the original. The tension arises when various individuals and groups stress the importance of the original, but the world seems to be inundated with well-hidden copies and forgeries.

The most overt instance of this dynamic is in the antique Americana market and the secretive, though lucrative, injection of forgeries into that market. The market thrives on rich Japanese connoisseurs ignorant of what differentiates the 'authentic' and the 'fake' antiques and artefacts; their interest lies in projections of 'authentic American culture' that can only be affirmed by outside experts such as Childan. Ironically, however, Childan's expertise is but middling: Frink shows himself to be much more knowledgeable than the antiques salesman, despite (and because of) being the originator of fakes and forgeries.

The necessity of outside experts is affirmed with Wyndam-Matson, who shows his tryst that while two cigarette lighters are as identical as they can be, one was used by FDR [Franklin Delano Roosevelt], and the other is but a copy of it — and he has papers which prove which is which. Wyndam-Matson notes that "The paper proves its worth, not the object itself" (p. 66).

A second layer of 'fakes' lies in personages. Frink, Joe, Baynes, and Abendsen, amongst others, all pretend to be people they are not, but there is no real way to prove their 'real' identities until the right authority claims to, or if they themselves reveal them. This dynamic particularly plays into the novel's analysis of Nazi racial paranoia, as space travel and Operation Dandelion appear to be the penultimate steps in what will become an 'ultimate holocaust' of all of humanity, ridding the Nazi war machine of the necessity of worrying whether secret Jews such as Frink exist at all. The Nazi solution to the blurring of the line between 'authentic' (Aryan) and 'fake' (Jewish) is to collapse the binary altogether through complete human destruction.

The opposite solution, which is not so much a solution as it is a recognition of the flimsiness of the 'real-unreal' dichotomy, rests in Juliana's analysis of the *I Ching* and *The Grasshopper Lies Heavy*. Once she discovers that the novel was written entirely using the *I Ching*, and that the novel likely constitutes the 'real world', she fully acquiesces to the philosophy that the *I Ching* emphasises: to humbly submit to the fate the world throws at you.

THE SCI-FI GENRE

While the novel's primary focus is not on futuristic technologies and how humans might live in a society inundated with them, *The Man in the High Castle* still indeed occupies the sci-fi genre. Germany in this alternate-history story has not only already flown to the moon, but also to Mars, with plans to go to other planets in the solar system, and this Nazi obsession with ubiquitous conquest undergirds the entire narrative. In addition, rocketry has enabled people to travel from separate countries within an hour.

Philip K. Dick's other novels project similar ideas regarding technology: it is so ubiquitous that it feels entirely natural. It also cannot be said to be an ever-positive upward progression wherein technology improves and thus society improves; technological progress in fact complicates social life.

A primary example of this complication of social life is in the ability of many people, such as Frink, to make copies of originals – an ability that is only really possible with (at the time) fairly futuristic industrial equipment. As noted in the prior section, the multiplicity of copies blurs the line between 'real' and 'unreal' to such an extent

WWII AND AXIS DOMINATION

Philip K. Dick clearly went to great pains to construct a world wherein the Axis powers – Germany, Japan and Italy the foremost amongst them – won WWII. American life has transformed significantly, with great swathes of the continent under either Japanese or German control, and occupying citizens of those countries declared, with unspoken authority, to be superior to the native population. There is extensive and labyrinthine politics between the two victorious countries, and Dick includes a long exegesis on the fictional war of succession within Germany for the chancellorship following the death of Hitler's successor,

Bormann. This war of succession includes actual historical figures, with Joseph Goebbels, the former Reich Minister of Propaganda in real-world Nazi Germany, eventually taking the position.

One of the outcomes of this complex alternate construction is an analysis of the cultural psychology of the Nazis and the Imperial Japanese. Dick, born in 1928, would have grown up through the entirety of WWII, turning 17 by the time it ended in 1945. *The Man in the High Castle* then seems to be his way of understanding what occurred in those turbulent years via an alternate history, one which allowed him to project the Nazi and Japanese aims into their inevitable conclusions.

The Nazi way of thinking is emblematised in Reiss, whose paranoia regarding hidden Jewish agents leads him to almost order a military attack on Abendsen's 'Castle'. Baynes, reflecting on the Nazis, thinks that "their thinking tends towards that Götterdämmerung. They may well crave it, be actively seeking it, a final holocaust for everyone" (p. 234). 'Götterdämmerung' refers to German mythology, specifically to the event wherein all the gods and all things are destroyed in a final battle with evil forces – an apt reference for a political group considering the annihilation of an entire country, Japan, with nuclear weapons.

Tagomi and Paul Kasoura exemplify the Japanese thought process. Kasoura, Childan realises, is subtly encouraging Childan to participate in the dissolution of his own culture – or, hopefully, to save it by resisting the American-capitalist urge to mass produce. Tagomi, raised a Buddhist and a devout follower of the *I Ching*, shows the more self-destructive outcome of such a rational, one-to-one exchange-driven mindset: with the discovery of Operation Dandelion and his own killing of two men to save only one, he spirals slowly into a depression. It is only after he discovers the 'balance' in Edfrank art, a balance which could only be achieved by the prodding of his countryman Kasoura, that he possibly begins to rise out of his negative mental state. Both of these men exhibit an introversion, emphasised by a Japanese culture which punishes those who show too much of their inner feelings.

FURTHER REFLECTION

SOME QUESTIONS TO THINK ABOUT...

- What is the importance of the difference between 'real' and 'fake', 'authentic' and 'forged'? Is there any importance to the distinction?
- What does Philip K. Dick accomplish with the creation of an alternate history — one wherein the Axis powers won WWII? What themes does he explore that he might have been unable to had he not created this alternate history?
- How does the novel consider the commercialisation and mass production of artistic works or historical artefacts?
- Though in the novel they never cross paths, Juliana and Frank Frink were once married. In what ways does their relationship shape the narrative structure?
- Although Frank Frink must disguise his Judaism in order to avoid persecution, in doing so he does still conform to a racial stereotype: that

Jews hide amongst the populace and control events from the shadows. With the racial biases several characters in the novel exhibit in mind, how do race and racism function in a world where the distinction between 'real' and 'fake' is blurred?

- Many of Philip K. Dick's novels deal with high-tech sci-fi inventions and futures, and while there are such aspects in *The Man in the High Castle*, their presence is muted in comparison with the focus on international and interne-cine conflict. To what end does Dick utilise sci-fi technology in this particular novel? What considerations seem to be made?
- The *I Ching*, or *The Book of Changes*, tells its querents how to shape and grasp their futures, as much as the book seems to shape that future itself. How does the novel explore fortune telling?
- How does the novel explore the relationship between past, present and future?

We want to hear from you!
Leave a comment on your online library
and share your favourite books on social media!

FURTHER READING

REFERENCE EDITION

- Dick, P. K. (2015) *The Man in the High Castle.* London: Penguin Classics.

ADAPTATIONS

- *The Man in the High Castle.* (2015-present) [Television show]. Frank Spotnitz, creator. USA: Amazon Studios.

MORE FROM BRIGHTSUMMARIES.COM

- Reading guide – *Do Androids Dream of Electric Sheep?* by Philip K. Dick.

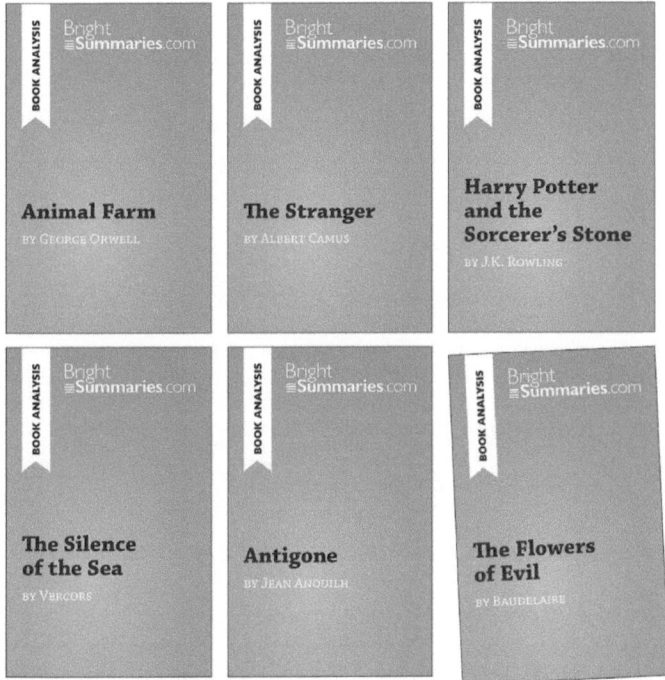

www.brightsummaries.com

Ebook EAN: 9782808019507

Paperback EAN: 9782808019514

Legal Deposit: D/2019/12603/142

Cover: © Primento

Digital conception by Primento, the digital partner of publishers.